WHAT DOES THE BIBLE SAY ABOUT

HELL?

Andrew Wommack

Published in partnership between Andrew Wommack Ministries and Harrison House Publishers.

Woodland Park, CO 80863 – Shippensburg, PA 17257

ISBN 13 TP: 978-1-59548-598-4

For Worldwide Distribution, Printed in the USA

1 2 3 4 5 6 / 26 25 24 23

Contents

Few people today believe hell is a real place. Even fewer believe anyone but the worst of all sinners are going there. There is a reason people don't believe in hell. It would affect their ability to live in sin (John 3:19–20). They don't want to be accountable for their actions.

It really doesn't matter what we believe or want. The important question is, what is true? Multitudes of people who don't believe in hell will wind up there regardless of how much they don't want it to be true. In this short booklet, I will share with you what God's Word says about hell. Jesus said God's Word is truth (John 17:17).

Denying the existence of hell or thinking only the worst of the worst go there are not biblical ideas. There is life after this life, and there are only two destinations possible: heaven or hell. It is only during this life that we get to choose our eternal destiny. Once we pass from this life, our fate is sealed. There will be no second chance.

I heard my first sermon on hell when I was only eight years old. The pastor shocked me by saying that there were good people in hell and bad people in heaven. I had assumed only bad people went to hell and all good people went to heaven. I thought if our good outweighed our bad, then we would go to heaven. But this pastor made it very clear that only forgiven people go to heaven, and all who don't accept salvation through faith in Jesus go to hell; and he started naming names.

> It is only during this life that we get to choose our eternal destiny.

I didn't respond right then, but when I got home, I couldn't wait to ask my dad about all of this. Praise the Lord, my dad was able to explain to me that *"all have sinned and come short of the glory of God"* (Rom.

3:23); and because of that, "*the wages of sin is death*" (Rom. 6:23a). But Jesus took our punishment of death and offered us eternal life if we would only believe on Him as our Savior (Rom. 6:23b; 2 Cor. 5:21; John 3:16; Rom. 10:9).

I knelt right there in my bedroom with my dad and received God's gift of salvation as an eight-year-old. No one can be saved unless they are willing to admit they've sinned and can't save themselves. Jesus only died for the ungodly (Rom. 4:5), so my first step towards salvation was to recognize my sinfulness; and that sermon on hell is what did it. Jesus said we have to repent of our sin, or we will perish (Luke 13:3–5). I repented of my sin and made Jesus my Lord and was saved (Rom. 10:9–13). I immediately received peace with God (Rom. 5:1).

This booklet is a brief synopsis of what the Bible has to say about hell. This probably isn't anyone's favorite topic, but it's the truth; and the truth will make you free (John 8:32). I encourage you to prayerfully consider these truths and let God's Word shape your beliefs and not our godless culture (Rom. 12:2).

What Does the Bible Say?

There are eighty-six verses in the Bible that mention hell by that name. That doesn't include the times the Hebrew word *Sheol* was translated "pit" or "grave" which also refers to hell. There are also other references to *damnation* and *perishing* and other passages referring to the effects of hell, which increase this number of scriptures greatly. There are literally hundreds of scriptures that deal with hell's reality.

Jesus said hell was created for the devil and his angels.

> *Then shall he say also unto them on the left hand, Depart from me, ye cursed, into everlasting fire, prepared for the devil and his angels.*

> Matthew 25:41

Hell wasn't part of the Lord's original plan for mankind. So, in a sense, anyone who goes to hell goes there against the Lord's original plan for them. His will is for no one to perish but that all would come to repentance (2 Pet. 3:9); but He doesn't force His will upon us (Deut. 30:19). We have to choose salvation by our own free will (Rom. 10:13).

One of the arguments against there being a hell is that it wouldn't be fair for the Lord to send people to hell who didn't even believe it exists. What about the people who have never heard teaching on hell? Would it be fair to hold them accountable?

No one will ever stand before God and be able to accuse Him of not warning them of hell. Inside of every person, God put an internal, intuitive witness of their sinfulness and need for salvation.

> Hell wasn't part of the Lord's original plan for mankind.

For the wrath of God is revealed from heaven against all ungodliness and unrighteousness of men, who hold the truth in unrighteousness; Because that which may be known of God is manifest in them; for God hath shewed it unto them. For the invisible things of him from the creation of the world are clearly seen, being understood by the things that are made, even his eternal power and Godhead; so that they are without excuse.

Romans 1:18–20

He literally puts thousands of obstacles in everyone's path to turn them from hell. Each of us has a conscience that convicts us of right and wrong.

Which shew the work of the law written in their hearts, their conscience also bearing witness, and their thoughts the mean while accusing or else excusing one another.

Romans 2:15

To wind up in hell, an individual has to go around thousands of roadblocks the Lord put in their way. They are without excuse!

When Adam and Eve sinned, they plunged the whole world into death and opened the door to hell for all their descendants. We became sinners through what Adam did. Our acts of sin just confirm the sin nature we inherited through Adam (Rom. 5:12–19). According to Ephesians 2:3, we are by nature the children of the devil (wrath) until we receive salvation through faith in what Jesus did for us. Then we become children of God with His nature inside us (Luke 20:36; Rom. 8:16–17).

Since all have sinned (Rom. 3:23), hell is the destination for all of mankind unless they repent and receive the salvation offered to them, only through Jesus (John 14:6; Acts 4:12).

There are seventeen biblical writers who spoke of hell. The One who spoke of hell the most is Jesus. Jesus said that unless we repent, we will all perish (Luke 13:3–5).

Hell is currently in the center of the earth (Matt. 12:30 and Eph. 4:9) and the residence of all who have died without receiving God's salvation through faith in Jesus. When the Lord creates a new heaven and a new earth, hell will be replaced by the lake of fire (Rev. 19:20; 20:10–15). That will be the place of torment throughout all eternity for those who don't receive salvation.

Memory vs. Forgetfulness

Jesus taught that hell is a place of torment and memory will be part of that torment:

*But Abraham said, Son, **remember** that thou in thy lifetime receivedst thy good things, and likewise Lazarus evil things: but now he is comforted, and thou art tormented.*

Luke 16:25

Compare that with what the Lord spoke through Isaiah about the righteous in the future creation:

For, behold, I create new heavens and a new earth: and the former shall not be remembered, nor come into mind.

Isaiah 65:17

Heaven will be so glorious that unlike the rich man in hell (Luke 16:19–31), all the sufferings of this life will never come to mind for those who are forever united with the Lord in heaven.

Paul confirmed this when he said,

For I reckon that the sufferings of this present time are not worthy to be compared with the glory which shall be revealed in us.

Romans 8:18

Heaven is a place where Jesus will wipe all tears away from our eyes, and there will be no more death, sorrow, crying, or pain (Rev. 7:17 and 21:4). In contrast to that glorious state, those in hell will be tormented with regrets, memories, constant pain, thirst, and suffering.

A Place of Torment

The rich man who went to hell in Jesus' parable said,

And in hell he lift up his eyes, being in torments, and seeth Abraham afar off, and Lazarus in his bosom. And he cried and said, Father Abraham, have mercy on me, and send Lazarus, that he may dip the tip of his finger in water, and cool my tongue; for I am tormented in this flame.

Luke 16:23–24

This reveals that hell will be torment, and part of that torment will be flames and thirst. In contrast to that, heaven will be a place where...

They shall hunger no more, neither thirst any more; neither shall the sun light on them, nor any heat. For the Lamb which is in the midst of the throne shall feed them, and shall lead them unto living fountains of waters: and God shall wipe away all tears from their eyes.

Revelation 7:16–17

> Heaven is a place where Jesus will wipe all tears away from our eyes.

What about Purgatory?

There is no mention in Scripture of what the Catholic Church calls "purgatory" or any intermediate dwelling place between this life and our eternal destiny (heaven or hell). On the contrary, Paul said in 2 Corinthians 5:8,

> *We are confident, I say, and willing rather to be absent from the body, and to be present with the Lord.*

Paul was speaking to believers and revealed that when our spirits leave our bodies (James 2:26), we are instantly present with the Lord. Notice that he was confident about this. Paul also spoke about his desire to depart this life and be with the Lord in Philippians 1:23. He didn't believe in a "soul sleep" or purgatory. When he left his body, he would be with the Lord.

The Lake of Fire

Hell is where all the ungodly dead currently go after this life. It is located in the center of the earth (Matt. 12:30; Eph. 4:9). At the end of this age, when the Lord creates a new heaven and a new earth, hell will be cast into "the lake of fire." That will be the eternal place of torment.

And the beast was taken, and with him the false prophet that wrought miracles before him, with which he deceived them that had received the mark of the beast, and them that worshipped his image. These both were cast alive into a lake of fire burning with brimstone.

Revelation 19:20

And the devil that deceived them was cast into the lake of fire and brimstone, where the beast and the false prophet are, and shall be tormented day and night for ever and ever.

Revelation 20:10

And I saw a great white throne, and him that sat on it, from whose face the earth and the heaven fled away; and there was found no place for them. And I saw the dead, small and great, stand before God; and the books were opened: and another book was opened, which is the book of life: and the dead were judged out of those things which were written in the books, according to their works.

Paul didn't believe in a "soul sleep" or purgatory.

13

And the sea gave up the dead which were in it; and death and hell delivered up the dead which were in them: and they were judged every man according to their works. And death and hell were cast into the lake of fire. This is the second death. And whosoever was not found written in the book of life was cast into the lake of fire.

Revelation 20:11–15

No Escape

Let's look again at the parable Jesus gave, about a rich man and a beggar named Lazarus in Luke 16:19–31. The rich man died and went to hell. The beggar died and was carried by the angels into Abraham's bosom, which Jesus called "paradise" in Luke 23:43. Both of these places were in the heart of the earth (Matt. 12:40; Eph. 4:9).

All who died before Christ's resurrection went to a place called Sheol (the Hebrew word for *pit* or *grave*). It was divided into two parts: paradise and hell. Between hell and paradise, or Abraham's bosom, as Jesus referred to it in the parable of the rich man, there was a great unpassable gulf separating the two (Luke 16:26). The rich man in hell could not escape.

The Revelation passages about hell also show there is no second chance. Our eternal fate is settled by the decisions made in this life. Once a person is committed to hell or later cast into the lake of fire, it is eternal.

> *The same shall drink of the wine of the wrath of God, which is poured out without mixture into the cup of his indignation; and he shall be tormented with fire and brimstone in the presence of the holy angels, and in the presence of the Lamb: And the smoke of their torment ascendeth up **for ever and ever**: and they have no rest day nor night, who worship the beast and his image, and whosoever receiveth the mark of his name.*

> Revelation 14:10–11

*And the devil that deceived them was cast into the lake of fire and brimstone, where the beast and the false prophet are, and shall be tormented day and night **for ever and ever**.*

Revelation 20:10

The writer of Hebrews also spoke of eternal damnation as one of the basic doctrines of the faith (Heb. 6:2). If the Lord cast angels who sinned down to hell, why would anyone think He would do any less with us (2 Pet. 2:4).

David said,

The wicked shall be turned into hell, and all the nations that forget God.

Psalm 9:17

Solomon spoke of the adulteress:

Her feet go down to death; her steps take hold on hell.

Proverbs 5:5

Her house is the way to hell, going down to the
chambers of death.

Proverbs 7:27

Solomon also warned anyone who would commit adultery:

But he knoweth not that the dead are there; and
that her guests are in the depths of hell.

Proverbs 9:18

Proverbs 27:20 says,

Hell and destruction are never full…

So, there is always room for anyone who chooses to go there.

Jesus said that anyone who calls his brother a fool is in danger of hell fire (Matt. 5:22). Jesus said that God the Father had the power to destroy both soul and body in hell (Matt. 10:28). Jesus said it would be better to lose a hand, foot, or eye than to be cast into hell in the next life (Matt. 18:8–9). He also warned that blaspheming the Holy Spirit would cause eternal damnation (Mark 3:29).

But the good news is that Jesus died for sinners (Rom. 5:8), and no one has to go to hell. There is a way—only one way—of escape.

The Proper Response

So, according to God's Word, heaven and hell do exist. One of these two destinations will be our eternal home. We can't wait until this life is over to make our choice. We have to choose now.

The choice is ours, but this really is a "no brainer." As the Lord inspired Moses to write in Deuteronomy 30:19:

> I call heaven and earth to record this day against you, that I have set before you life and death, blessing and cursing: therefore choose life, that both thou and thy seed may live.

The Lord gives each one of us the choice, but just in case you aren't sure if life or death is the right choice, the Lord gave you the answer to this quiz by saying, "choose life." The Lord doesn't want anyone to go to hell. He loved you so much He sent Jesus to the earth to bear your sins and pay your debt (John 3:16).

> **Jesus died for sinners, and no one has to go to hell.**

Someone might ask, "Why is God so set against sin? What's the big deal?" It's because God is just and holy. In Him is no sin (1 John 3:5). He would cease to be just if He just decided to not hold people's sins against them. His holiness and justice will not allow Him to just look the other way. Rom. 6:23a says,

> *The wages of sin is death...*

Sin has a payment that has to be paid. The Lord told Adam that if he sinned, he would die (Gen. 2:17), and God cannot lie (Heb. 6:18). Every word that comes out of His mouth is a covenant or contract (Ps. 89:34). It's the integrity of God's Word that holds the universe together (Heb. 1:3). If He ever lied, the universe would self-destruct.

So, there was a debt, and for God to be holy and true to His word, that sin debt had to be paid. But because God is also love (1 John 4:8, 16), He made a way for us to escape the damnation of hell. He sent His only begotten son to become a man and bear our punishment. Jesus not only suffered the agonizing death of crucifixion, but he went to hell for you and me (Eph. 4:9–10).

Jesus paid our debt so we could go free, but it has to be received. The Lord gave mankind a free will. He doesn't force anyone to believe on Him. His Holy Spirit draws us (John 6:44), but we have to choose.

Romans 10:9 says,

That if thou shalt confess with thy mouth the Lord Jesus, and shalt believe in thine heart that

*God hath raised him from the dead, thou shalt
be saved.*

It really is that simple. Jesus paid our debt and offers total freedom to us as a gift. That's what the second part of Romans 6:23 says:

*For the wages of sin is death; but the **gift** of God
is eternal life through Jesus Christ our Lord.*

Salvation through faith in what Jesus did for us is a gift to be received and not a wage to be earned. If we got what we deserved, every one of us would go to hell. But Jesus offers forgiveness to anyone who will call on His name for salvation (Rom. 10:13).

Jesus said that He was the only way to relationship with God.

*Jesus saith unto him, I am the way, the truth,
and the life: no man cometh unto the Father,
but by me.*

John 14:6

Acts 4:12 says,

Neither is there salvation in any other: for there is none other name under heaven given among men, whereby we must be saved.

If you have never humbled yourself before God and repented of your sins, I invite you to do that now. The payment for your sins has already been made through Jesus (1 John 2:2). There is no doubt about whether or not God will accept you. He said in Romans 10:13,

> If we got what we deserved, every one of us would go to hell.

For whosoever shall call upon the name of the Lord shall be saved.

The only question is, will you accept Him?

Pray this prayer with me:

"Father God, I acknowledge that I've sinned and

need your forgiveness. I believe Jesus died and took the punishment for my sin. I make Jesus my Lord and Savior. I now believe and receive the forgiveness that Jesus provided. I am forgiven, and I welcome You to come and live in me. Thank You for my new life with You and redeeming me from hell. Help me to love and serve You all my days. Amen!"

If you prayed that and meant it from your heart, you are now what Jesus called, "born again" or "born from above." (John 3:3–6). You are a brand-new person in Christ. Your new life has just begun. There is much to learn, and I would love to help you get started.

We have a free book that I would love to send to you. I have over 200,000 hours of free teaching on my website: **awmi.net**. We also have a 24/7 Helpline with people who would love to rejoice with you over your decision to receive salvation. They will pray with you and help you in any way they can. The number is **(719) 635-1111**.

Scriptures about Hell

1. Hell is a real place.

"The wicked shall be turned into hell, and all the nations that forget God." Psalm 9:17

"Let death seize upon them, and *let them go down quick into hell: for wickedness* is *in their dwellings,* and *among them."* Psalm 55:15

"If I ascend up into heaven, thou art *there: if I make my bed in hell, behold, thou* art there." Psalm 139:8

"Her house is *the way to hell, going down to the chambers of death."* Proverbs 7:27

"But he knoweth not that the dead are *there;* and that *her guests* are *in the depths of hell."* Proverbs 9:18

"Hell from beneath is moved for thee to meet thee *at thy coming: it stirreth up the dead for thee,* even *all the chief ones of the earth; it hath raised up from their thrones all*

the kings of the nations. Yet thou shalt be brought down to hell, to the sides of the pit." Isaiah 14:9, 15

"I made the nations to shake at the sound of his fall, when I cast him down to hell with them that descend into the pit: and all the trees of Eden, the choice and best of Lebanon, all that drink water, shall be comforted in the nether parts of the earth. They also went down into hell with him unto them that be *slain with the sword; and* they that were *his arm,* that *dwelt under his shadow in the midst of the heathen."* Ezekiel 31:16–17

"Though they dig into hell, thence shall mine hand take them; though they climb up to heaven, thence will I bring them down." Amos 9:2

"And fear not them which kill the body, but are not able to kill the soul: but rather fear him which is able to destroy both soul and body in hell." Matthew 10:28

"And if thine eye offend thee, pluck it out, and cast it *from thee: it is better for thee to enter into life with one eye,*

rather than having two eyes to be cast into hell fire."
Matthew 18:9

"And if thy hand offend thee, cut it off: it is better for thee to enter into life maimed, than having two hands to go into hell, into the fire that never shall be quenched: Where their worm dieth not, and the fire is not quenched. And if thy foot offend thee, cut it off: it is better for thee to enter halt into life, than having two feet to be cast into hell, into the fire that never shall be quenched: Where their worm dieth not, and the fire is not quenched. And if thine eye offend thee, pluck it out: it is better for thee to enter into the kingdom of God with one eye, than having two eyes to be cast into hell fire: Where their worm dieth not, and the fire is not quenched. For every one shall be salted with fire, and every sacrifice shall be salted with salt." Mark 9:43–49

"And in hell he lift up his eyes, being in torments, and seeth Abraham afar off, and Lazarus in his bosom."
Luke 16:23

"Because thou wilt not leave my soul in hell, neither wilt thou suffer thine Holy One to see corruption." Acts 2:27

"For thou wilt not leave my soul in hell; neither wilt thou suffer thine Holy One to see corruption." Psalm 16:10

"Wherefore he saith, When he ascended up on high, he led captivity captive, and gave gifts unto men. (Now that he ascended, what is it but that he also descended first into the lower parts of the earth?)" Ephesians 4:8–9

"For if God spared not the angels that sinned, but cast them down to hell, and delivered them into chains of darkness, to be reserved unto judgment." 2 Peter 2:4

"And death and hell were cast into the lake of fire. This is the second death." Revelation 20:14

2. It's a place of eternal torment.

"Whose fan is in his hand, and he will throughly purge his floor, and gather his wheat into the garner; but

he will burn up the chaff with unquenchable fire."
Matthew 3:12

"Wherefore if thy hand or thy foot offend thee, cut them off, and cast them from thee: it is better for thee to enter into life halt or maimed, rather than having two hands or two feet to be cast into everlasting fire." Matthew 18:8

"Then shall he say also unto them on the left hand, Depart from me, ye cursed, into everlasting fire, prepared for the devil and his angels. And these shall go away into everlasting punishment: but the righteous into life eternal." Matthew 25:41, 46

"But he that shall blaspheme against the Holy Ghost hath never forgiveness, but is in danger of eternal damnation." Mark 3:29

"And if thy hand offend thee, cut it off: it is better for thee to enter into life maimed, than having two hands to go into hell, into the fire that never shall be quenched: Where their worm dieth not, and the fire is not quenched.

And if thy foot offend thee, cut it off: it is better for thee to enter halt into life, than having two feet to be cast into hell, into the fire that never shall be quenched: Where their worm dieth not, and the fire is not quenched. And if thine eye offend thee, pluck it out: it is better for thee to enter into the kingdom of God with one eye, than having two eyes to be cast into hell fire: Where their worm dieth not, and the fire is not quenched. For every one shall be salted with fire, and every sacrifice shall be salted with salt." Mark 9:43–49

"*Of the doctrine of baptisms, and of laying on of hands, and of resurrection of the dead, and of eternal judgment.*" Hebrews 6:2

"*Even as Sodom and Gomorrha, and the cities about them in like manner, giving themselves over to fornication, and going after strange flesh, are set forth for an example, suffering the vengeance of eternal fire.*" Jude 1:7

"*And the smoke of their torment ascendeth up for ever and ever: and they have no rest day nor night, who worship the beast and his image, and whosoever receiveth the mark of his name."* Revelation 14:11

"And the devil that deceived them was cast into the lake of fire and brimstone, where the beast and the false prophet are, and shall be tormented day and night for ever and ever. And I saw a great white throne, and him that sat on it, from whose face the earth and the heaven fled away; and there was found no place for them. And I saw the dead, small and great, stand before God; and the books were opened: and another book was opened, which is the book of life: and the dead were judged out of those things which were written in the books, according to their works. And the sea gave up the dead which were in it; and death and hell delivered up the dead which were in them: and they were judged every man according to their works. And death and hell were cast into the lake of fire. This is the second death. And whosoever was not found written in the book of life was cast into the lake of fire." Revelation 20:10–15

3. Hell is full of fire and brimstone.

"Whose fan is in his hand, and he will throughly purge his floor, and gather his wheat into the garner; but he will burn up the chaff with unquenchable fire." Matthew 3:12

"But I say unto you, That whosoever is angry with his brother without a cause shall be in danger of the judgment: and whosoever shall say to his brother, Raca, shall be in danger of the council: but whosoever shall say, Thou fool, shall be in danger of hell fire." Matthew 5:22

"Wherefore if thy hand or thy foot offend thee, cut them off, and cast them from thee: it is better for thee to enter into life halt or maimed, rather than having two hands or two feet to be cast into everlasting fire. And if thine eye offend thee, pluck it out, and cast it from thee: it is better for thee to enter into life with one eye, rather than having two eyes to be cast into hell fire." Matthew 18:8–9

"Then shall he say also unto them on the left hand,

Depart from me, ye cursed, into everlasting fire, prepared for the devil and his angels." Matthew 25:41

"And if thy hand offend thee, cut it off: it is better for thee to enter into life maimed, than having two hands to go into hell, into the fire that never shall be quenched: Where their worm dieth not, and the fire is not quenched. And if thy foot offend thee, cut it off: it is better for thee to enter halt into life, than having two feet to be cast into hell, into the fire that never shall be quenched: Where their worm dieth not, and the fire is not quenched. And if thine eye offend thee, pluck it out: it is better for thee to enter into the kingdom of God with one eye, than having two eyes to be cast into hell fire: Where their worm dieth not, and the fire is not quenched. For every one shall be salted with fire, and every sacrifice shall be salted with salt." Mark 9:43–49

"And in hell he lift up his eyes, being in torments, and seeth Abraham afar off, and Lazarus in his bosom. And he cried and said, Father Abraham, have mercy on me,

and send Lazarus, that he may dip the tip of his finger in water, and cool my tongue; for I am tormented in this flame." Luke 16:23–24

"Even as Sodom and Gomorrha, and the cities about them in like manner, giving themselves over to fornication, and going after strange flesh, are set forth for an example, suffering the vengeance of eternal fire." Jude 1:7

"The same shall drink of the wine of the wrath of God, which is poured out without mixture into the cup of his indignation; and he shall be tormented with fire and brimstone in the presence of the holy angels, and in the presence of the Lamb. "And the smoke of their torment ascendeth up for ever and ever: and they have no rest day nor night, who worship the beast and his image, and whosoever receiveth the mark of his name." Revelation 14:10–11

"And the beast was taken, and with him the false prophet that wrought miracles before him, with which he deceived them that had received the mark of the beast,

and them that worshipped his image. These both were cast alive into a lake of fire burning with brimstone." Revelation 19:20

"And the devil that deceived them was cast into the lake of fire and brimstone, where the beast and the false prophet are, and shall be tormented day and night for ever and ever." Revelation 20:10

"But the fearful, and unbelieving, and the abominable, and murderers, and whoremongers, and sorcerers, and idolaters, and all liars, shall have their part in the lake which burneth with fire and brimstone: which is the second death." Revelation 21:8

Biblical Characters Who Spoke of Hell

Moses

"For a fire is kindled in mine anger, and shall burn unto the lowest hell, and shall consume the earth with her increase, and set on fire the foundations of the mountains." Deuteronomy 32:22

David

"*The sorrows of hell compassed me about; the snares of death prevented me.*" 2 Samuel 22:6

"*The wicked shall be turned into hell, and all the nations that forget God.*" Psalm 9:17

"*If I ascend up into heaven, thou art there: if I make my bed in hell, behold, thou art there.*" Psalm 139:8

Zophar (Job's friend)

"*It is as high as heaven; what canst thou do? deeper than hell; what canst thou know?*" Job 11:8

Job

"*Hell is naked before him, and destruction hath no covering.*" Job 26:6

Solomon

"*Her feet go down to death; her steps take hold on hell.*" Proverbs 5:5

"Her house is the way to hell, going down to the chambers of death." Proverbs 7:27

"But he knoweth not that the dead are there; and that her guests are in the depths of hell." Proverbs 9:18

"Hell and destruction are before the LORD: how much more then the hearts of the children of men? The way of life is above to the wise, that he may depart from hell beneath." Proverbs 15:11, 24

"Thou shalt beat him with the rod, and shalt deliver his soul from hell." Proverbs 23:14

"Hell and destruction are never full; so the eyes of man are never satisfied." Proverbs 27:20

Isaiah

"Therefore hell hath enlarged herself, and opened her mouth without measure: and their glory, and their multitude, and their pomp, and he that rejoiceth, shall descend into it." Isaiah 5:14

"Hell from beneath is moved for thee to meet thee at thy coming: it stirreth up the dead for thee, even all the chief ones of the earth; it hath raised up from their thrones all the kings of the nations. Yet thou shalt be brought down to hell, to the sides of the pit." Isaiah 14:9, 15

"And your covenant with death shall be disannulled, and your agreement with hell shall not stand; when the overflowing scourge shall pass through, then ye shall be trodden down by it." Isaiah 28:18

"And thou wentest to the king with ointment, and didst increase thy perfumes, and didst send thy messengers far off, and didst debase thyself even unto hell." Isaiah 57:9

Ezekiel

"I made the nations to shake at the sound of his fall, when I cast him down to hell with them that descend into the pit: and all the trees of Eden, the choice and best of Lebanon, all that drink water, shall be comforted in the nether parts of the earth. They also went down into

hell with him unto them that be slain with the sword; and they that were his arm, that dwelt under his shadow in the midst of the heathen." Ezekiel 31:16–17

"And they shall not lie with the mighty that are fallen of the uncircumcised, which are gone down to hell with their weapons of war: and they have laid their swords under their heads, but their iniquities shall be upon their bones, though they were the terror of the mighty in the land of the living." Ezekiel 32:27

Amos

"Though they dig into hell, thence shall mine hand take them; though they climb up to heaven, thence will I bring them down." Amos 9:2

Jonah

"And said, I cried by reason of mine affliction unto the Lord, and he heard me; out of the belly of hell cried I, and thou heardest my voice." Jonah 2:2

Habakkuk

"Yea also, because he transgresseth by wine, he is a proud man, neither keepeth at home, who enlargeth his desire as hell, and is as death, and cannot be satisfied, but gathereth unto him all nations, and heapeth unto him all people." Habakkuk 2:5

Jesus

"But I say unto you, That whosoever is angry with his brother without a cause shall be in danger of the judgment: and whosoever shall say to his brother, Raca, shall be in danger of the council: but whosoever shall say, Thou fool, shall be in danger of hell fire." Matthew 5:22

"And fear not them which kill the body, but are not able to kill the soul: but rather fear him which is able to destroy both soul and body in hell." Matthew 10:28

"And thou, Capernaum, which art exalted unto heaven, shalt be brought down to hell: for if the mighty works, which have been done in thee, had been done in Sodom, it would have remained until this day." Matthew 11:23

"And I say also unto thee, That thou art Peter, and upon this rock I will build my church; and the gates of hell shall not prevail against it." Matthew 16:18

"Wherefore if thy hand or thy foot offend thee, cut them off, and cast them from thee: it is better for thee to enter into life halt or maimed, rather than having two hands or two feet to be cast into everlasting fire. And if thine eye offend thee, pluck it out, and cast it from thee: it is better for thee to enter into life with one eye, rather than having two eyes to be cast into hell fire." Matthew 18:8–9

"Ye serpents, ye generation of vipers, how can ye escape the damnation of hell?" Matthew 23:33

"Then shall he say also unto them on the left hand, Depart from me, ye cursed, into everlasting fire, prepared for the devil and his angels. And these shall go away into everlasting punishment: but the righteous into life eternal." Matthew 25:41, 46

"And if thy hand offend thee, cut it off: it is better for thee to enter into life maimed, than having two hands

to go into hell, into the fire that never shall be quenched: Where their worm dieth not, and the fire is not quenched. And if thy foot offend thee, cut it off: it is better for thee to enter halt into life, than having two feet to be cast into hell, into the fire that never shall be quenched: Where their worm dieth not, and the fire is not quenched. And if thine eye offend thee, pluck it out: it is better for thee to enter into the kingdom of God with one eye, than having two eyes to be cast into hell fire: Where their worm dieth not, and the fire is not quenched. For every one shall be salted with fire, and every sacrifice shall be salted with salt." Mark 9:43–49

"And in hell he lift up his eyes, being in torments, and seeth Abraham afar off, and Lazarus in his bosom. And he cried and said, Father Abraham, have mercy on me, and send Lazarus, that he may dip the tip of his finger in water, and cool my tongue; for I am tormented in this flame. But Abraham said, Son, remember that thou in thy lifetime receivedst thy good things, and likewise Lazarus evil things: but now he is comforted, and thou

art tormented. And beside all this, between us and you there is a great gulf fixed: so that they which would pass from hence to you cannot; neither can they pass to us, that would come *from thence. Then he said, I pray thee therefore, father, that thou wouldest send him to my father's house: For I have five brethren; that he may testify unto them, lest they also come into this place of torment. Abraham saith unto him, They have Moses and the prophets; let them hear them. And he said, Nay, father Abraham: but if one went unto them from the dead, they will repent. And he said unto him, If they hear not Moses and the prophets, neither will they be persuaded, though one rose from the dead."* Luke 16:23–31

Peter

"Because thou wilt not leave my soul in hell, neither wilt thou suffer thine Holy One to see corruption." Acts 2:27 (with Psalm 16:10)

"For if God spared not the angels that sinned, but cast them down to hell, and delivered them into chains of darkness, to be reserved unto judgment." 2 Peter 2:4

Paul

"*Wherefore he saith, When he ascended up on high, he led captivity captive, and gave gifts unto men. (Now that he ascended, what is it but that he also descended first into the lower parts of the earth?)*" Ephesians 4:9

"*And for this cause God shall send them strong delusion, that they should believe a lie: That they all might be damned who believed not the truth, but had pleasure in unrighteousness.*" 2 Thessalonians 2:11–12

Writer of Hebrews

"*Of the doctrine of baptisms, and of laying on of hands, and of resurrection of the dead, and of eternal judgment.*" Hebrews 6:2

James

"*And the tongue is a fire, a world of iniquity: so is the tongue among our members, that it defileth the whole body, and setteth on fire the course of nature; and it is set on fire of hell.*" James 3:6

Jude

"*Even as Sodom and Gomorrha, and the cities about them in like manner, giving themselves over to fornication, and going after strange flesh, are set forth for an example, suffering the vengeance of eternal fire.*" Jude 1:7

John

"*I* am *he that liveth, and was dead; and, behold, I am alive for evermore, Amen; and have the keys of hell and of death.*" Revelation 1:18

"*And the sea gave up the dead which were in it; and death and hell delivered up the dead which were in them: and they were judged every man according to their works. And death and hell were cast into the lake of fire. This is the second death. And whosoever was not found written in the book of life was cast into the lake of fire.*" Revelation 20:13–15

FURTHER STUDY

If you enjoyed this booklet and would like to learn more about some of the things I've shared, I suggest my teachings:

1. *Eternal Life*
2. *The New You & The Holy Spirit*
3. *Spirit, Soul & Body*
4. *A Sure Foundation*
5. *What Is Truth?*

These teachings are available either free of charge at **awmi.net/video, awmi.net/audio,** or for purchase in book, study guide, CD, DVD, or USB formats at **awmi.net/store**.

Receive Jesus as Your Savior

Choosing to receive Jesus Christ as your Lord and Savior is the most important decision you'll ever make!

God's Word promises, *"That if thou shalt confess with thy mouth the Lord Jesus, and shalt believe in thine heart that God hath raised him from the dead, thou shalt be saved. For with the heart man believeth unto righteousness; and with the mouth confession is made unto salvation"* (Rom. 10:9–10). *"For whosoever shall call upon the name of the Lord shall be saved"* (Rom. 10:13). By His grace, God has already done everything to provide salvation. Your part is simply to believe and receive.

Pray out loud: "Jesus, I acknowledge that I've sinned and need to receive what you did for the forgiveness of my sins. I confess that You are my Lord and

Savior. I believe in my heart that God raised You from the dead. By faith in Your Word, I receive salvation now. Thank You for saving me."

The very moment you commit your life to Jesus Christ, the truth of His Word instantly comes to pass in your spirit. Now that you're born again, there's a brand-new you!

Please contact us and let us know that you've prayed to receive Jesus as your Savior. We'd like to send you some free materials to help you on your new journey. Call our Helpline: **719-635-1111** (available 24 hours a day, seven days a week) to speak to a staff member who is here to help you understand and grow in your new relationship with the Lord.

Welcome to your new life!

Receive the Holy Spirit

As His child, your loving heavenly Father wants to give you the supernatural power you need to live a new life. *"For every one that asketh receiveth; and he that seeketh findeth; and to him that knocketh it shall be opened... how much more shall* your *heavenly Father give the Holy Spirit to them that ask him?"* (Luke 11:10–13).

All you have to do is ask, believe, and receive! Pray this: "Father, I recognize my need for Your power to live a new life. Please fill me with Your Holy Spirit. By faith, I receive it right now. Thank You for baptizing me. Holy Spirit, You are welcome in my life."

Some syllables from a language you don't recognize will rise up from your heart to your mouth (1 Cor. 14:14). As you speak them out loud by faith, you're releasing God's power from within and building yourself up in the spirit (1 Cor. 14:4). You can do this whenever and wherever you like.

It doesn't really matter whether you felt anything or not when you prayed to receive the Lord and His Spirit. If you believed in your heart that you received, then God's Word promises you did. *"Therefore I say unto you, What things soever ye desire, when ye pray, believe that ye receive* them, *and ye shall have* them*"* (Mark 11:24). God always honors His Word—believe it!

We would like to rejoice with you, pray with you, and answer any questions to help you understand more fully what has taken place in your life!

Please contact us to let us know that you've prayed to be filled with the Holy Spirit and to request the book *The New You & the Holy Spirit*. This book will explain in more detail about the benefits of being filled with the Holy Spirit and speaking in tongues. Call our Helpline: **719-635-1111** (available 24 hours a day, seven days a week).

Call for Prayer

If you need prayer for any reason, you can call our Helpline, 24 hours a day, seven days a week at **719-635-1111**. A trained prayer minister will answer your call and pray with you.

Every day, we receive testimonies of healings and other miracles from our Helpline, and we are ministering God's nearly-too-good-to-be-true message of the Gospel to more people than ever. So, I encourage you to call today!

About the Author

Andrew Wommack's life was forever changed the moment he encountered the supernatural love of God on March 23, 1968. As a renowned Bible teacher and author, Andrew has made it his mission to change the way the world sees God.

Andrew's vision is to go as far and deep with the Gospel as possible. His message goes far through the *Gospel Truth* television program, which is available to over half the world's population. The message goes deep through discipleship at Charis Bible College, headquartered in Woodland Park, Colorado. Founded in 1994, Charis has campuses across the United States and around the globe.

Andrew also has an extensive library of teaching materials in print, audio, and video. More than 200,000 hours of free teachings can be accessed at **awmi.net**.

Endnotes

1. David Barton, "Biblical Literacy," (presentation, Truth & Liberty Coalition Conference), September 9, 2022, accessed February 13, 2023, https://www.gospeltruth.tv/watch/?list=63175dbee9b2410001716d5c&id=631bc00dccd4240001f7e429.

2. "Pastors Face Communication Challenges in a Divided Culture," Barna Research Group, January 29, 2019, accessed February 21, 2023, https://www.barna.com/research/pastors-speaking-out/.

3. *Brown-Driver-Briggs Hebrew and English Lexicon*, s.v. "הָגָה" ("haga"), accessed February 13, 2023, https://www.blueletterbible.org/lexicon/h1897/kjv/wlc/0-1/.

4. *Thayer's Greek-English Lexicon of the New Testament*, s.v. "σπορά" ("spora"), accessed February 16, 2023, https://www.blueletterbible.org/lexicon/g4701/kjv/tr/0-1/.

5. *Thayer's Greek-English Lexicon of the New Testament*, s.v. "σπέρμα" ("sperma"), accessed February 16, 2023, https://www.blueletterbible.org/lexicon/g4690/kjv/tr/0-1/.

6. Laura Clark, "Tree Grown From 2,000-Year-Old Seed Has Reproduced," *Smithsonian Magazine*, March 26, 2015,

accessed February 21, 2023, https://www.smithsonianmag. com/smart-news/tree-grown-2000-year-old-seed-has-reproduced-180954746/.

7. *Strong's Exhaustive Concordance*, s.v. "αὐτόματος" ("autómatos"), accessed March 27, 2023, https://www. blueletterbible.org/lexicon/g844/kjv/tr/0-1/.

Contact Information

Andrew Wommack Ministries, Inc.

PO Box 3333
Colorado Springs, CO 80934-3333
info@awmi.net
awmi.net

Helpline: 719-635-1111 (available 24/7)

Charis Bible College

info@charisbiblecollege.org
844-360-9577
CharisBibleCollege.org

For a complete list of all of our offices,
visit **awmi.net/contact-us**.

Connect with us on social media.

Andrew's
LIVING COMMENTARY BIBLE SOFTWARE

Andrew Wommack's *Living Commentary* Bible study software is a user-friendly, downloadable program. It's like reading the Bible with Andrew at your side, sharing his revelation with you verse by verse.

Main features:
- Bible study software with a grace-and-faith perspective
- Over 26,000 notes by Andrew on verses from Genesis through Revelation
- *Matthew Henry's Concise Commentary*
- 11 Bible versions
- 2 concordances: *Englishman's Concordance* and *Strong's Concordance*
- 2 dictionaries: *Collaborative International Dictionary* and *Holman's Dictionary*
- Atlas with biblical maps
- Bible and *Living Commentary* statistics
- Quick navigation, including history of verses
- Robust search capabilities (for the Bible and Andrew's notes)
- "Living" (i.e., constantly updated and expanding)
- Ability to create personal notes

Whether you're new to studying the Bible or a seasoned Bible scholar, you'll gain a deeper revelation of the Word from a grace-and-faith perspective.

Purchase Andrew's *Living Commentary* today at **awmi.net/living**, and grow in the Word with Andrew.

Item code: 8350

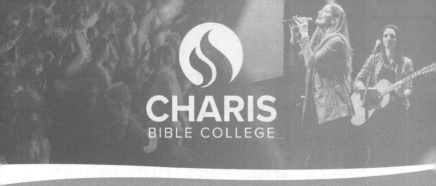

CHARIS
BIBLE COLLEGE

God has more for you.

Are you longing to find your God-given purpose? At Charis Bible College you will establish a firm foundation in the Word of God and receive hands-on ministry experience to **find, follow,** and **fulfill** your purpose.

Scan the QR code for a free Charis teaching!

CharisBibleCollege.org
Admissions@awmcharis.com
(844) 360-9577

Change your life. **Change the world.**

Your peace doesn't have to ebb and flow with the tides of circumstance. Build your life on the solid foundation of the Word.

Visit our website for teachings, videos, testimonies, and other resources that will encourage you with truth for any situation and help you learn God's plan for relationships, finances, faith, and more.

"I was lost deep in the world. . . . I started seeking the truth, and through AWM's resources, I have been set free . . . including receiving miracles of finances when everything seemed impossible. I am at peace with myself. I thank AWM for sharing the truth, which has freed me to understand God."

— David M.

Be empowered to live the victorious life God intended for you! Visit **awmi.net** to access our library of free resources.

Teaching God's unconditional love and grace.

Don't miss
The Gospel Truth
with Andrew Wommack!

Discover God's unconditional love and grace
and see God in a whole new way!

- ▶ Hear the Word of God taught
  with simplicity and clarity.

- ▶ Understand the true Gospel
  message and be set free
  from all kinds of bondages.

- ▶ Learn how to receive
  your breakthrough.

Go to **awmi.net/video** for local
broadcast times or to watch online.